Do You Think Teaching is Easy?

How to Relate, Facilitate, and Survive Your Way Through a Fabulous Teaching Career

By

Stephanie Smith

ISBN: 1-4107-3886-8 (e-book)
ISBN: 1-41073885-X (Paperback)
ISBN: 1-4107-3884-1 (Hardcover)

Library of Congress Control Number: 2003092596

This book is printed on acid free paper.

Printed in the United States of America
Bloomington, IN

1stBooks - rev. 04/24/03

Table of Contents

Introduction

In education, as in most professions, there are hidden rules that you will rarely learn from a textbook or from a class. Learning these important, but often silent, guidelines is usually accomplished by obtaining a teaching position and arriving at work on a daily basis. A teacher can deliver instruction with great success; however, if he/she is not privy to the hidden rules of the field, he/she is likely to experience great frustration with the teaching profession.

This book allows you to become familiar with two broad areas that will help you develop your teaching career. The first section is dedicated to how you relate to others, whether it is an administrator, a teacher, a parent, or the public. The second section highlights specific job duties that challenge teachers on a daily basis. The final section addresses your personal needs as you begin your career; namely, your physical, mental, emotional, and spiritual health.

It is my hope that you find this book to be your launching pad. At the end of each subsection, there is a brief list of questions. Over time and experience, your answers will change. In the years to come, your willingness to keep an open heart and a flexible attitude will be rewarded not only in the success of your students, but in your ability to hand the baton of teaching to the next generation.

Section I: Relating

Relating with others effectively is a requirement for success in every career. There are numerous relationships that must be cemented for an individual, a department, or an organization to run well. The field of education is no exception. From students to parents to administration, this is a profession that requires plenty of people skills. I have learned more about relating to people in my ten years in education than in my high school and college years combined. Throughout those ten years, I have maintained several long-term friendships and have kept my list of enemies small.

If you have this book in your hands, you are most likely already an educator or you are quickly headed in that direction. If you are to remain in this field and enjoy it, there are five types of relationships that you must master. The following sections will assist you in forming and maintaining working relationships with administrators, teachers, students, parents, and the public.

Chapter 1: Relating to Administrators

Once you have applied to a district, successfully completed preliminary interviews, and have turned in your paperwork, your name will be thrown into a pile greatly appreciated by principals everywhere. Often, teachers turn in resignations or requests for transfers a couple of months prior to the end of the school year. However, due to various circumstances, the principal may be informed of a change just before the start of a new year. In either case, the school administrator must consider staffing needs. Understandably, he/she wants the most qualified person available for each open position.

Somewhere on your journey to the classroom, you will be interviewed by the school administrator. In some schools, you may find yourself being interviewed by a team of school personnel. This could include assistant principals, grade level chairs, and/or the teachers that would be on your team if you should be offered the position. The reason for this interviewing team is not to scare or to intimidate you. On the contrary, it is to allow other campus team members to buy in to you. The campus administrator likes nothing better than to have a peaceful campus. If everyone involved agrees that you are the best person for the position, you are more likely to be received with open arms by your new peers.

Although everyone else may like you, the final decision is usually based on the desires of the administrator. The principal recommends you to the district and, most of the time, the rest is history. It is important that you understand what that recommendation means. It means that the principal trusts you with the lives of children. It means that he/she trusts you to keep state test scores at an excellent status. Most of all, it means that the administrator is expecting you to walk into that classroom and give 200% every day.

The new teachers that become quickly successful are the ones who are willing to learn. They are like sponges ready to soak up every bit of advice given to them. Although not all advice is perfect, they learn to take the good, to weed out the bad, and to derive greatness from both.

Most administrators will not directly lean over your shoulder each day to ensure that you are doing your job. Instead, they often rely on team leaders (or grade level chairs) to oversee your growth. An effective grade level chair will meet with his/her team on a regular basis, will do what they can to assist new teachers, and will plan with their team as much as possible.

Most likely, you will find that other seasoned teachers on your team are helpful as well. Each teacher will have his/her own slant on issues, but you can learn from all of them. You will find that your relationships with the other teachers will indirectly affect your relationship with your campus administrator. The administrator has come to trust the abilities of these teachers over time. The administrator has learned their strengths and utilizes them for both the success of the students and the campus. If your communication within your new team is positive, the administrator will likely see you as a team player. If, on the other hand, you are constantly opposing folks, in disagreement with everything being done, not pulling your weight as a team member, or acting as if you are the incoming expert, you will most likely find yourself ostracized by all, including the administrator. There will be times when you disagree with others; you may even have a valid point. However, remember to be respectful. Some of your cohorts may have opened the doors of that campus. They may have prevailed through many difficult years. Remember to honor the blood, sweat, and tears of others as you begin your own journey in this very challenging field.

Once you build relationships with your coworkers, you may begin to feel confident in your job and in your beliefs about how you should teach. It is at this stage that a teachable heart becomes critical. If you are to continue to grow, you must remain teachable and respectful of others.

Unfortunately, the principal is the person that I see most often disrespected by educators who need to remain teachable. Throughout my career, I have witnessed teachers who argue with the principal, both in private and in front of other staff members. Some people are not quite that brazen.

Instead, they rally their troops and begin to downgrade the principal to folks throughout the hallways. Ironically, these same people expect their students to treat them with the utmost honor. Although you may not always agree with every decision that the principal makes, try to see the issue from that person's point of view. A campus administrator is much like the middle of a sandwich. Under the administrator are students and teachers. These two groups have unique needs and wants. Often forgotten about by both of these groups is upper administration. These folks also make demands of the principal. Above them is a host of laws and procedures that the principal must adhere to. Last but not least, the principal must be available to parents. The principal must make decisions based on the big picture. They must ask themselves, "What is best for all students and adults involved?"

All of the demands are sure to make a principal busy. Although you will be busy too (only seeing the restroom once in a while), your principal is probably one of the most overwhelmed of campus personnel. The one question that probably resounds in his/her sleep is, "Oh, Mr. /Ms._____, do you have a minute?" If they look like they really are not interested, you may not need to take it personally. They may just NOT have a minute to give. However, effective administrators will often give you the minute that they do not have or will ask you to see them at an alternate time if you have questions or concerns.

There will be situations where you will desperately need the support of your administrator. Whether it is the angry parent, the constantly disruptive student, or the staff member that is driving you insane, you will find yourself, at some point, in the principal's office seeking wisdom and direction. Be faithful to complete the tasks given to you. If he/she gives you a deadline, meet it. If he/she gives you safe and legal advice, follow it. If he/she gives you a mandate, abide by it. In most situations, principals will do their best to reciprocate when the situation arises.

After being in the profession for a while, you may begin to see teaching as a thankless job. At least you will have the opportunity to deal with some positive people. Often, the principal only sees parents and community members who are disgruntled in some way. Most effective principals must adopt the philosophy of praising the staff when something is successful, but taking personal responsibility when something goes wrong. If you see a campus that is successful, thank the teachers and support staff that are making it possible, but always remember to be appreciative of a self-sacrificing leader.

As a new teacher, I viewed the position of Principal as one of great honor, to be filled by someone who had neared perfection as an educator. Over time, I became frustrated when I felt that my superiors were not supportive of me when students, parents, or colleagues were challenging me. I remember one afternoon several years ago when I was especially tempted to quit. A student with severe behavior problems had made a negative choice in my classroom; it was one of several throughout the day. I sent him to the office and was told, "It is 2:30 p.m. Why can't you just hold on to him for 30 minutes?" The worst part was that it was said in front of the child. There he sat, grinning at my loss of authority.

Fortunately for my career, I have learned that administrators are people, capable of mistakes and frustration. I have enjoyed observing as principals lead teachers, students, and their communities in a path of educational success. Indeed, they are not perfect. However, successful principals gracefully cover any perceived weakness with great professional strength. As my career developed, I have discovered that teachers must display similar power in the classroom.

It is important that a Principal supports the teachers as much as possible; however, it is essential that the teacher supports him/herself. As time progressed, I began to care for my career in the truest professional sense. I documented student behavior in a legal manner. I made positive statements to parents before making negative ones. I also quit sending students to the office. The minute a student left my classroom upon my request, I believe that I conveyed a destructive message: "I have no authority over you. Please find someone who does." I had just relinquished the power of my position to someone else. If a student is out of control, it may be necessary to isolate them for safety purposes. Therefore, you may find it necessary to send a student to the office. If so, create your own plan. Send that student with an assignment that they have to complete before returning. Have the student call his/her parents in your presence. Do something to let that student know that you are still in control. The student will sense the presence of your authority and the Principal will appreciate your efforts.

1. What will I be able to contribute to this position that will make the administrator glad to have recommended me?

2. Will my administrator be able to trust me to do my job? (Will I meet deadlines and adhere to administrative mandates?)

3. Am I willing to be a team player? In what ways do I believe that I am or that I can be a team player?

4. What will I do to remain teachable?

5. How can I sincerely encourage others, including my campus administrator?

Chapter 2: Relating to Teachers

It was my first year of employment in a new school district. Although I had taught before, I was acquiring the skills for teaching a different grade level. Report cards were due at the end of the first six weeks. I shared students with other teachers, so I sent my students to their next destination at the end of class, report cards in hand. (Each teacher filled out the grade for his/her content area.) During my next class, another teacher busted into my room and, in front of my students, said, "WE DO NOT FILL OUT REPORT CARDS THIS WAY!"

After this surprising introduction to the new campus, I also had several teachers who offered to help me in any way that they could. It was not long before the teacher that was my next door neighbor was also one of my best friends.

15

This teacher was a few years older than I. Although I had been teaching longer, she had life experiences to share that I quickly learned to value and to appreciate. She and I began sharing ideas with one another, sharing stories about our personal lives, and then remaining friends through the trials and tribulations of teaching. She and I have both left the district, but we remain close friends. I think that a best friend may be the survival secret to teaching. If you have a buddy, you are more likely to endure difficult experiences with great strength.

Through the years, I have learned to love and appreciate all teachers for one reason or another. They come in multiple ages and stages. The stage that they are in says something about what they are able to give.

There are teachers who have been in the classroom for many years. They may have the exact same bulletin board presentation that they used twenty years ago or they may continue to learn, grow, and change with the tide. At least in some areas, these teachers remain steadfast on certain issues. Although you may consider them to be less than fresh material, I have come to appreciate them for the unconditional love that they usually display upon children. They seem to know how to deal with unruly students, challenging parents, and can even make an administrator think twice before speaking. They may be extremely sweet but they may also be the perfect one to help you deal with a student behavior issue. If they seem harsh or unfriendly, appreciate their good points anyway. They may have an ill family member, financial issues, concerns about retirement, or they may just be tired from a lifetime of service. Befriend them. Learn from them. They are usually a rare and priceless package of wisdom.

The group of teachers that follow are what I call the "slightly seasoned". They have several years of experience, but are usually not the elders of the group. If they remain teachable and do an effective job, they are usually well respected by others. They may gain opportunities to be grade level chairs and to serve on various committees along with the well-seasoned folks. They have enough knowledge to be of great benefit to an administrator and they are often at various turning points in their lives. They may be considering having a family, raising a family, taking on new leadership roles, and they may be deciding on just how far they would like to take their career. This decision may require returning to school, taking additional certification tests, and managing their time extremely well so as to meet the needs of their jobs, their families or other personal commitments, as well as their personal needs.

It is also at this point when teachers decide to either be a team player or to just shut their door and teach. Although in times past, teachers were able to decide on the latter, external and internal mandates are requiring educators to work in a unified effort. Those who meet this challenge with enthusiasm are often granted various leadership roles. As a new teacher, I used to watch these people and wonder if I would ever be one of them. Now, here I am. A few scrapes, plenty of laughs, and a few tears later, I am now "slightly seasoned". It is a wonderful place to be. I can still learn from the elders, but I am able to assist those new to the field. It is as if I am holding hands with two sides of Heaven. If you keep a teachable heart and a positive attitude, you will wake up one morning and find that you are in this wonderful place as well.

There is another group of teachers whose dynamics have changed a great deal in the past few years. They are the new teachers. In recent history, most teachers were prepared by traditional professional educator programs offered by colleges and universities. Teachers completed their course of study and came to their first jobs with strong beliefs regarding the way that a classroom should be handled and the way that they should teach children. Often, these ideals differed with the campus status quo. This resulted in either the teacher compromising his/her views to fit the needs of the campus or it caused the other folks to view teaching in a new light, especially if the new style proved effective for students. Usually, a healthy combination took place. The new teacher came with enthusiasm and a readiness both to utilize the fresh ideals, as well as zeal to learn about what works from those with experience.

However, there is now a different type of new teacher that many schools are just learning how to mentor. Whether it is someone who has worked in another field or someone newly out of college, teachers with alternative certifications present a new and different challenge to those who wish to see them succeed. In the traditional circumstance, it was taken for granted that the new teacher was aware of the basics of the field of education. With a great need for teachers in populated areas, districts are often in need of people who are alternatively certified (usually meaning that they have a degree in something other than education). Although alternative certification programs do their best to provide training that will make these new teachers successful, much more on-the-job support is sometimes needed. The value of alternatively certified personnel lies in their expertise of their individual fields of study. They bring varied knowledge and career choices to the classroom; this can ultimately result in benefiting the future of students. The two truths that I have learned most from new teachers is their willingness to try different strategies and techniques (and to try again with a different slant if it fails) and their positive attitude when it comes to learning from others. Whether traditionally or alternatively certified, one fact remains true; teaching is not for the weak. It is for those who are willing to endure encouragement and discouragement, praise and criticism, long term success gained by temporary failure.

1. What do I want to learn from the well seasoned educator? How can I benefit from his/her expertise?

2. What can I gain from the slightly seasoned teacher? How can I show appreciation and respect toward teachers at all levels?

3. How can I befriend other new teachers? How can I encourage them to grow?

Chapter 3: Relating to Students

The first time that a student called me by name, I realized that, for a few hours each day, I was the center of someone's world of learning. Someone actually trusted me to pass the gift of knowledge on to them. What an awesome responsibility! Although it is unlikely that students will willingly sit at your feet to gain great amounts of knowledge and wisdom from you with open hearts and respectful behavior, I have always found great satisfaction in my ability to make a curriculum come alive to students and to see them enjoy learning. Now, it is your turn!

Once you have obtained a position, completed necessary paperwork, and have seen your classroom for the first time, you may experience a sense of euphoria as you realize that you are now a teacher. The euphoria is usually packaged with stress as you prepare for the most important part of your new job—teaching your students. If you are beginning a new school year with your students, everyone is freshly prepared for a new experience. However, if you take a job during the school year, you may have special challenges to face, depending on the history of that classroom. Some classes have had multiple substitutes while others have had a committed teacher that left for a personal reason. Either way, this is where your journey truly begins.

Depending on the grade level that you teach, you may encounter teenagers attempting to find their position in a peer group (At various times, this takes great precedence over learning.). You may experience students who have never parted from their parents before and you must decide how to handle that particular situation.

Whatever grade level you teach, learn basic policies and procedures of the campus prior to entering the classroom with your students. Also, ask other teachers around you how they handle the first day of school. Remember, you know more than your students and they are no doubt just as nervous as you are in many cases.

Whether it is the first day or the last day of school, be sure that your students have something to do when they walk in. Down time equals off-task behavior, which equals insanity for you. Aside from starting the day (or the class period), your greatest challenge will be transition times, moving from one activity to another. My personal philosophy is to conquer in small groups. If you are asking younger children to move from one part of the room to another, ask three or four students to move at a time. If dealing with older students, explain all procedures prior to requesting follow-through. Basically, when you are a new teacher, it is best to plan every minute of the day and then some. It is better to plan extensively than to not plan enough.

If you are walking into this career thinking that children will be the same as they were when you were in school, you might consider rethinking. With the advances in technology and in the general pace of our world, even the average 4-year-old is not the same as a 4-year-old ten years ago. If you are to gain the interest of your students, you will have to compete with electronics and a fast moving world to do so.

However, teachers are wonderful at being creative, at changing techniques to match the times, and at making learning fun for everyone. Utilize technology. Always relay to your students how they can use what you teach in a real world situation.

When motivating students to learn, it is important to do just that—motivate them! Give them encouragement. Have an "I know you can do it!" attitude. In essence, catch them being good and encourage them to excel.

There will be days when you feel like giving up because students are challenging. You will question what to do with them. You may not feel supported. You may feel like shedding a few tears. But take courage! You may want to keep a journal as a personal friend for those rough days. When you write things, problems are often clarified and solved easier. Try to decide what the factors were that caused the off-task behavior and consider what changes you can make the next day. Try several strategies. Ask advice from another teacher that you trust. If necessary, have a parent conference (it is perfectly alright to ask another teacher to sit in with you during your first few parent conferences).

Whatever you do, involve the student. Young people have minds, too. Conduct a conference with the child. Bring the child in on the parent conference. Respect them as people. A teacher's positive relationship with a student can inspire that child for the rest of his/her life. (Sadly, a negative relationship can have an equal, but harmful, negative effect.) You do not want to be friends with your students, but you do want to love them. Do everything you are able to do for the students in your classroom and when the year is over, you will feel successful because you have given your greatest effort...and that will make you a great teacher!

1. How can I balance firmness with love toward my students?

2. How can I motivate my students to learn?

3. What skills (social, academic, emotional) do I want my students to leave with at the end of the school year?

Chapter 4: Relating to Parents

In my years of teaching, I have encountered enough parents (and various types of parents) that I could write a book on this subject alone. Parents are as varied as the students that sit in your classroom. Some parents approached me with upfront support, stating at the beginning of the year that if their child made bad choices in class, I was to call them and that they would take care of the problem immediately. Other parents were angry with me when confronted with their child's behavior. Still others are rarely involved at all. In some cases; however, I believe that a parent can be overly involved. Some parents choose to make their child the center of their world. When this happens, every move of the teacher is carefully scrutinized so as not to damage the child for life. Sadly, the child is often smothered, never being allowed to lead their own life (to an age-appropriate extent). Through it all, I have found that many parents are supportive and positive toward the teacher. I have often enjoyed the displays of appreciation at the end of a school year for having taught their child and for having made a positive impression for learning throughout the school year. Parents, like all of us, are busy and often overwhelmed by life. When they take the time to thank you, you can be sure that it is from the heart.

One event that has remained with me regarding parents took place a couple of years ago. When teaching small children, I love to see them become as independent and as responsible as possible because it gives them the confidence to grow as a person. A Mother insisted on doing things for her child that her child was well able to do independently. I made my request known, but kept my peace afterward. A couple of weeks later, the parent reported to me that her child had decided that he wanted to do things for himself and that she should let him do so.

Whether they are angry or not, appreciative or not, support parents as much as possible. Most of the time, you will only have one year with your students. Whatever you do or say, make it a great year for them.

Successful communication with parents requires the skills of a customer service expert. In some ways, the students are your main customers because you are providing them with an education. In another sense, parents are also customers. Parents who love their children want them to have the best education possible. Once you walk into the classroom, you realize that you have a tall order to fill, especially where parents are concerned.

The grade that you teach is directly correlated to the amount of parent involvement that will be required of you, in most cases. Secondary education tends to have less parental interaction than do their elementary counterparts. Whereas in high school, students may make their own decisions regarding schedules and elective courses, the Pre-Kindergarten or Kindergarten students are often accompanied by parents to the classroom. (Sometimes, the student cries. Other times, the parent cries. Still in other situations, both rejoice!)

Regardless of the student's age, know that the parents are entrusting you with their most precious gifts. Although children may present a challenge at times, they are held dear in the hearts of their parents. Parents of younger children may seem apprehensive at first. The professional educator should not take this personally. Instead, send home an information packet about your classroom. You may want to include what you will be studying during the first couple of weeks. The more information that a parent is given, the greater their comfort level will be. Make future newsletters bright and cheery to reassure the parents that their child is in a positive environment.

By all means, find something great about each student and tell the parents about it. Everyone loves to hear something good about their child. This will also be of great assistance to you in case you need to tell them something less positive later. Compliment your students to their parents as often as possible. This should make the year's parent/teacher relationship a success.

For many reasons, parent conferences are often necessary. They may be district required, you may want to get to know your parents in this way, or there may be an academic or a behavioral concern. Never have a parent conference in an isolated situation, regardless of the subject of discussion. If you feel confident enough to have a conference without another teacher present, make sure that someone is around in case you need them (preferably another professional). Perhaps you and a teacher across the hall might schedule parent conferences during the same time periods, ensuring that you will both be available if either of you should need assistance.

Early in my teaching career, I had scheduled parent conferences after school when very few people were around. My classroom was located in a portable building in the back of the campus. I was scheduled to conference with a single father. He was extremely nice and seemed proud of his son's progress. He began complimenting me to a point that was somewhat inappropriate. It was only later that I realized what a horrible situation that could have been.

In the last few years, I have witnessed a new concern rising among educators. Parents sometimes come to the school with a negative attitude, perhaps because of a previous experience that took place when they were in school, or because of current stresses, or both. I have witnessed parents who yell, use obscene language, and make physical contact with the teacher or the principal. This should never be tolerated. Police or district security is usually contacted in these cases. Whatever the challenge, try to remain calm. If you remain calm and in control of your own actions, parents will usually become less aggressive when they realize that they are truly being listened to. Whether having someone near as a quick information reference or as a safety buddy, it is best to have other professionals in close proximity when dealing with parents.

Prior to interactions with parents, decide how much personal information that you are comfortable sharing with them. Although many parents may never ask you a personal question, some parents attempt to interview you, asking you how long you have taught, what previous experience that you have had, where you live, and how many children you have. Most parents just want to know that their child is with someone who is safe and who loves kids. However, it is usually best to keep some information private. Parents who know that it is your first year to teach may attempt to blame all of their child's problems on you being new as opposed to making their child responsible for their own behavior. If they know that you are new to the field, be sure to highlight your previous experiences with children. Any other information that you give is up to you. The rule of thumb is to not give out more information than you are comfortable giving. For example, some new teachers attempt to befriend parents by giving them a home or a cell number. They usually learn the necessity for a professional distance when a parent does not respect boundaries and calls them during inappropriate times of the day and night.

Parents should be seen as customers, just as your students. They are individuals for whom you are providing a service. However, as in any profession, you can be friendly without being friends. In order for you to successfully teach and to have a personal life, boundaries must be set. At the beginning of the year, parents should be informed regarding when you will conference with them and when you will return phone calls. In the past, I have always provided my parents with the school's main number. They left messages and I returned their calls during my planning period or after school.

1. How will I make positive comments to my parents as soon as possible (notes, calls, etc.)?

2. How can I schedule my conferences so that others will be in close proximity? Do I have someone who is willing to be my conference buddy?

3. How can I prepare myself to deal with an angry parent?

4. What personal information should remain personal?

5. How can I make myself available to parents, yet establish appropriate boundaries?

Chapter 5: Relating to the Public

Soon after I obtained my first teaching position, there was a campus retirement party for a member of the custodial staff. During the party, I saw an attractive woman making her way through this social maze called a party and visiting with various school personnel. I thought that it was great that this custodian's wife was so supportive of him. I walked toward her and introduced myself, then added the comment, "Congratulations on your husband's retirement!" To my embarrassment, I learned that she was not his wife; rather, she was one of the teaching staff. I was fortunate that this was actually a humorous event. Relating to the public is its own art form. As educators, we are public servants. We interact with our community on a continual basis. It is our duty to ensure that the community views us and our campus in a positive light, with our demeanor as well as our achievements.

Schools are not only a place for educating students. They are also a place to vote, a place to hold community meetings or church services, and they may also be attractive to the press if there is a story needing to be covered. In essence, school campuses are also houses for a plethora of community programs and projects.

There are a few important tips when dealing with the public. To begin with, if you see a stranger lurking in the halls, you should ask him/her if he/she has been to the office and obtained a visitor's pass. (This is how the campus is able to keep record of who is in the building. Voting or other special programs are usually contained to one specific area, giving visitors little reason to prowl through the hallways.) Although some folks are parents requesting to pick their child up early, there have also been plenty of cases of stolen purses or school belongings at the hands of wandering strangers. At all times, safety for the students should take precedent over a visitor's convenience.

What if you find yourself in the hall needing to deal with a disruptive student? You may be a wonderful teacher, but if someone off the street sees you correcting a student, they may see it as mistreatment. A good rule is to keep a low voice at all times with students. As opposed to yelling from afar, walk toward the student and correct him/her in a private tone. The student will not need to save face in front of others by acting out more and you will have saved yourself possible heartache.

When dealing with the public, think about the people that you interact with at the bank, at the grocery store, or at the doctor's office. Do you like them to be pleasant and professional? Keep in mind that you are representing your school and that outsiders appreciate a pleasant, polite demeanor.

If you should ever encounter a member of the press, do not give out information. Know your district's procedures regarding the press. Most districts have specified personnel to deal with the press, whether that is a public relations expert from central office or whether it is your campus administrator. Whatever the situation, you probably do not have all of the facts. It is best to let those identified persons make comments to the press after all facts have been gathered.

1. What should I do if someone unfamiliar is in the hall without a visitor's pass?

2. What are some creative ways that I can quietly deal with disruptive students both in and out of the classroom?

3. How should I represent our school when dealing with the public?

4. What is my district's policy regarding what I should/should not say to the press?

Section II: Facilitating

The field of education needs effective facilitators. I believe that an effective facilitator is one who knows how to motivate people, to manage his/her time well, and who possesses some type of organization in which he/she accomplishes a task. There are at least five broad areas for which the teacher is usually responsible: classroom management, lesson plans, paperwork and deadlines, evaluations, and professional liability. To fail in any of these areas is to put yourself at risk of losing your new career. To succeed in all of these is to continue on your journey toward excellence as an educator.

The following chapters will address each of these specifically. My hope is to provide you with a broad overview of what will be expected of you as an educator.

Regardless of the state, the district, or the grade-level, handling these tasks in a timely and professional manner should give you a necessary boost as you enter the classroom.

Chapter 6: Classroom Management

Although I briefly touched on this subject while discussing your relationship with your students, I will address it again here in more detail. If a new teacher feels like a failure, it is usually because of student behavior in the classroom. In a way, I could share hours worth of wisdom regarding this challenge, yet in another way, any advice is of little assistance until you get in there and gain the wealth of wisdom from your own experience.

Probably the greatest piece of knowledge that I can share is that it is impossible to control another person. You will not be able to control your students. You will not be able to control whether or not you have support from their parents. You will not have much power over whether your administrator is supportive of you. The person that you can always control is you!

If you were in control of your students, then all of their negative behavior would be your fault. It is not. They make the choice of whether or not to follow rules. They make the choice regarding whether or not they will learn. You have a choice of whether you will be reactive or proactive. Reactive teachers are those folks who constantly react to student behavior. They usually wait until a student does something wrong and then respond negatively to the action. Consequently, students are rarely motivated to learn because they are only given negative attention. Proactive teachers catch students doing something right and react to the positive. When negative consequences are necessary, the student is held responsible. He/she knows the rules of the classroom, sometimes makes a choice not to follow them, but is aware of the consequence prior to the action.

To begin your year, display a brief list of classroom rules. Make the rules positive statements. For example, rather than saying, "Do not hit anyone", you may want to say, "Use self control." This rule covers broad territory and refrains from giving the students any creative ideas for negative actions.

Although there are many resources on student discipline and classroom management, a good rule is to treat all students equal. Whatever encouragements you give for positive actions and whatever negative consequences that follow misbehavior, remain fair and consistent. Students at any age can sense favoritism or partiality and will resent you for it, even if they are on the receiving end of your good graces.

Some schools have a generic discipline plan in place. If your campus has such a program, familiarize yourself with it. Otherwise, talk to several teachers from your grade level, as well as from other grade levels. You will gain a variety of ideas and can fit them together to best suit your own style.

One of the most important aspects of classroom management is modeling. A teacher who models the social skills that he/she desires to see in students will cause the students, in most cases, to begin to reflect that behavior. In other words, only ask your students to do what you are willing to do.

1. What are five ways that you can be proactive in the area of classroom management?

2. What are three positively stated rules that will address the management needs of my classroom?

3. What are at least five ways that I can be fair to all students throughout the day (boys and girls, multicultural groups of students, etc.)?

4. How can I model the social skills that I want my students to reflect throughout the school year?

Chapter 7: Lesson Plans

Every accomplished task is preceded by a plan, whether thought or written. In education, the blueprint of teaching is the lesson plan. If it is formulated correctly, it should produce a classroom filled with constant learning. Lesson plans that are weakly developed are calls for catastrophes, both in teaching and in classroom management. Formats of lesson plans are as varied as the teachers who create them and the administrators that require them.

Whether your school chooses your lesson plan format or whether you create your own is not as important as what it contains. An excellent lesson plan will include the following; an objective, a means of assessment, and the materials required. The mistake that teachers sometimes make is to see a cute activity and throw it into their lesson plans. All lesson plans should be a means to an end. What skill (s) do you want your students to take with them into the real world as a result of what you are teaching? The answer to this question should be found in your objective. For example, a teacher may want the students to know how to use "borrowing" in subtraction. The written objective might say, "The student will be able to apply their knowledge of borrowing (place value) in order to balance a teacher-made checkbook register." This objective is clearly stated, telling anyone who may read it that students will not only learn how to borrow, but how they will apply it to a real world situation. The means of assessment is stated as well. The teacher could make a pretend checkbook register with several entries and a beginning balance. The students could use their knowledge of borrowing to obtain a correct balance. (This is the end result of a successful lesson. If students are unable to master this skill, the need for re-teaching the concept is apparent.) This objective lends itself to what materials will be necessary, at least for the assessment. Whatever materials that the teacher finds necessary to teach the concept of borrowing should be specifically listed in the lesson plan, especially if you are a new teacher. A lesson plan can be magnificently written, but if teaching materials are not in place, a great deal of learning time is lost.

If your school has a previously set lesson plan format, ask to see other teachers' lesson plans. This will give you specific ideas regarding how to write your own. (Your grade level chair is usually a great person to ask.) If your school does not have a specific format, go ahead and ask to see others' plans. You can still gain an important foundation for building your own style.

Some administrators ask that your lesson plans be turned in. Others do not. Whatever the case, ask your administrator and, if you need to turn them in, know the deadline. It is a good idea to share your first few plans with another teacher that you trust to be constructively critical, whether or not you are required to turn them in. Many schools now offer a mentor. Sometimes, these mentors are located on the campus while others float from campus to campus as a district representative. These are also great people to share your plans with.

1. How can I learn to write specific, effective objectives during my first year of teaching?

2. How can I assess students in order to know that they have mastered a skill?

3. What are some ways that I can organize and manage materials in the classroom and in my lesson plans so that I make the most out of my instructional time?

4. Who do I feel comfortable asking to assist me with lesson plans? Do I have a mentor? How often are they available for helping me with various issues?

Chapter 8: Paper Work and Deadlines

During my student teaching experience, I was allowed to sit in on several Admission, Review, and Dismissal (ARD) meetings for special needs children for the purpose of training. After attending a few meetings, I had learned a little about the process and was excited when I was allowed to take an active role. One afternoon, there was an ARD that lasted well over 1.5 hours. Finally, everyone signed the paperwork and last minute details were being accomplished. I was asked to "tear the papers". The school diagnostician looked pale when she saw me about to rip the first page into two pieces. She quickly grabbed the page and modeled for me what she meant. She wanted me to tear off the carbon copies and group them according to the color of the sheets.

After that day, I always remembered what tearing the papers really meant.

If you have attended school or been an employee at any time in your life, you are no stranger to paper work and deadlines. It is a fact of life in our modern society. Education is no exception. As the demand for accountability increases, so does our need for organization as educators. Specific to teaching is the need for paper work in the areas of government funded programs as well as the management of the local campus and district.

The financial support of the federal government toward education is wrapped up in the federal programs available on the local campus. These programs include but are not limited to Special Education, Bilingual and ESL education, Head Start, and Compensatory Education. If you are a general education teacher, some of your students may receive no government programs while others may attend speech. Still others may attend a special education class. If you are a specialized teacher, your salary may be at least partially funded by the federal government.

In any case, paperwork is necessary for accurate documentation. Whether the paperwork includes the amount of time that services are offered to the student per school year or a list of modifications needed to make the student successful in the regular classroom, the fact that funding is utilized properly should be well documented.

During the years that I taught special education, I was largely responsible for the paperwork for each of the students in my class. Each time that there was an annual ARD, I was responsible for at least seventeen pages of paperwork per individual child. While teaching general education, I found myself responsible for only a couple of pages once the child began receiving services. However, as inclusion becomes paramount, the general education teacher, in some cases, is taking on a more meaningful role in every child's education. If you have students who are receiving any type of extra services, be sure that you are aware of what paperwork you are responsible for, if any, and know when it has to be completed. It is a good idea that you have someone more experienced than you assist with legal paperwork while you are familiarizing yourself with the process of that particular district.

In addition to legal paper work, you may also be faced with forms related to the school or the district. These usually have deadlines, as well. You will also encounter specific campus projects as you join committees and get involved in campus life as a teacher.

When you receive a lesson plan format and a grade book, you should also consider a day-timer. It is important that you have some type of calendar at your fingertips, whether traditional or technological. In order to keep abreast of deadlines, projects, meetings, and student deadlines, you must be organized! Decide on a calendar layout that works for you, then sleep, eat, and breathe with it throughout the school year.

1. I am already teaching. Here is a list of my students receiving special services as well as what type of services they are receiving:

2. This is a list of the paperwork that I am responsible for on each of the students mentioned above:

3. What is my plan regarding meeting my paperwork and project deadlines, as well as attending necessary meetings faithfully?

Chapter 9: Teacher Evaluation

Early in my career, I taught young children and had prepared an evaluation lesson centered on a famous tale. In order to ensure student focus, I painted my face like a pig, complete with a snout. My first question was, "How many of you think that I look like a pig?" The students laughingly raised their hands, but in retrospect, I am happy that I did not ask that question of older students. In all of my years of teaching, I have never completely mastered the natural nervousness of being evaluated. I have learned to laugh at myself and to do the best job that I possibly can. After all, that is the limit to what anyone can ask. Evaluation is a serious matter. However, you can improve your performance by being the best teacher that you can be, every day of the year.

In every job, there is performance evaluation. In most jobs, evaluation of an employee consists of looking at their performance and skills as a team member over the past year. The evaluation of a teacher is somewhat different. Your campus administrator must come in and observe you while teaching for a specified amount of time. Depending upon your state's method of evaluation, there is usually some type of self-evaluation report that you must complete as well.

Although your evaluation may not be directly linked to salary increases, it is linked to job security. School districts need highly qualified teachers in the classroom. As a nation, our public education system is being held to a higher level of accountability. The districts must have quality teachers in order to uphold high standards of instruction and learning.

Prior to your evaluation, ask to have a pre-evaluation conference with your campus administrator. Discuss any students who have discipline issues. Also, ask the administrator what he/she is looking for in an observation. Take notes if you wish. Be familiar with your state's evaluation system. Either someone on the campus or at the district level should be able to answer any questions. You can also contact the governing body of your state's education system.

During your evaluation, relax. Be sure that you always have quality lessons planned and materials prepared. In doing so, you will always have an effective learning environment for students and you will be prepared for any evaluations, whether they are announced or not. Teach as you usually do on any given day. Anything other than the normal will cause anxiety in the students, which will create undue stress for you. The change will be extremely obvious to anyone observing you.

If you want to do an active, hands-on lesson for your evaluation, use an active approach as much as possible throughout the year. Students learn best when given real world experiences (as opposed to only a reading assignment and questions to answer). Your students will be confident, independent, and willing to challenge themselves. You and your class will be well on the road to excellence.

When the evaluation is over, you should have an opportunity to discuss your evaluation with your administrator. This is a perfect time to debrief with your principal regarding your teaching practices. Rather than asking him/her what you can improve on, make a note of areas for improvement prior to the conference. Make a list of strategies that you can use for your own improvement and growth (training, reading, attempting new strategies in the classroom, observing other teachers, etc.). Discuss the areas of desired improvement with your administrator and suggest a plan of action for growth. Ask for feedback regarding your plan. Make special note of his/her response. Most likely, your principal will appreciate the fact that you took the time to self-evaluate and that you are willing to continue to grow professionally.

1. What about being evaluated makes me anxious? What will I say to my administrator regarding my concerns during our pre-conference?

2. How can I teach throughout the school year to ensure both successful students and a successful evaluation?

3. In what areas do I need continued professional growth? What is my plan of action to accomplish this?

Chapter 10: Professional Liability

We have all heard the reports of the liability issues prevalent in the medical profession. However, those who work in the area of health are no longer alone. Many professionals now find themselves dealing with liability issues on a daily basis. Education is also extremely impacted by the threat of lawsuits or other legal consequences. Districts usually have full or part time attorneys whom they can depend on for legal advice, as well as for legal defense when necessary.

Just as it is important for a doctor to have personal liability insurance, it is important for educators to gain financial protection. Educators' Associations usually offer liability insurance to teachers. Shop around for the amount of liability that the various associations offer. Make a note of due amounts. Most dues can be withdrawn from your check on a monthly basis. Whether you choose an association or a private insurance, be sure to protect yourself in the event of judicial action taken against you.

There is one word that will save you from much heartache: documentation. Few wish to bother with it until a catastrophe takes place. Afterward, the educator will usually document for the rest of his/her career. Keep a notebook near your desk. The notebook could include but is not limited to phone conference logs, a pocket for notes from parents and returned notes signed by parents, a parent conference log, and a student behavior log. Your grade book, report cards, and student cumulative data should serve as adequate documentation for academics. However, all phone and person-to-person conferences with parents should be documented. Include what the conversation was regarding, as well as plans of action agreed upon by you and the parent (s). Record any areas of disagreement. The date of the conference should be recorded. As for student behavior, include the date, exactly what the student said or did as well as any action taken on your part. If it involved other students, this should be documented as well. When documenting, be objective. State only what happened; do not include any opinions, whether others or your own.

In order to prevent lawsuits, be sensible. Know your campus procedures regarding discipline, emergency situations, and dealing with parents and the public. Follow that procedure to the letter. If you are unsure in any situation, ask someone reliable. If a child is hurt or possibly ill, send the student to the nurse. The nurse will document the visit. Be sure that students are monitored at ALL times. If not, you are putting yourself at risk by being neglectful.

Stephanie Smith

During a fire drill or when going from one place to another, make sure that all of your students are with you.

Whether you are on duty or in your classroom, always monitor students carefully. Talking to another adult can quickly take your mind away from students. Thus, students are free to make wrong choices, hurting themselves and others, and causing you a liability issue. When you are neglectful, you are limiting the amount of protection that your campus administrator and your district can provide.

One area that is often neglected when discussing issues of liability is copyright. There should be someone on your campus or in your district who can assist you with these issues. You may wish to consult your school librarian first. Whatever you have in your possession, know whether or not you have the right to copy it, whether from a traditional or technological source.

1. How will I obtain liability coverage for myself as a professional?

2. What else do I need to learn about documentation? Who can I ask? How will I organize my documentation?

3. What are some sensible things that I can do on a daily basis to avoid liability issues?

4. Who will I ask if I have a question regarding copyright?

Stephanie Smith

Section III: Surviving

In any career, survival is the basis of everything from relating to people to facilitating your work. In order to be successful, we must survive physically, mentally, emotionally, and spiritually. We must survive in both our relationships with others, as well as with ourselves. To neglect any of these areas is to sabotage our efforts. We cannot give to others what we do not already have within us. As you read the following chapters, may you find peace with yourself, with others, and with your chosen career.

Stephanie Smith

Chapter 11: Physical Health

My first major experience with professional education was student teaching. I was acquiring both a certification in regular and in special education. My student teaching experience lasted one semester and was split between those two fields.

As I grew in experience, I found that my waistline grew as well. If there were treats left by the PTA in the teacher's lounge, I would sample. I would eat when I first arrived home, eat supper, and then snack before retiring to bed. In one semester, I gained thirty pounds.

As I grow older (now at the ripe old age of 32), I have realized just how much we eat for emotional reasons. I was rarely eating out of a physical need for hunger. I ate because I had given all day. I had given my instruction to children, my planning period to parents and my lunch time to endless phone calls to people who were rarely home. I desperately needed a few moments in my day when I did nothing. Eating became my escape from stress. Between making unhealthy eating choices at times and having a tiring job, I never had the strength (or the commitment to myself) to exercise when I arrived home. This provided me with even less energy.

I did not have to be a physician to see myself sliding down a spiral, quickly. Knowing that stress encourages me to eat, I have two choices: I can substitute eating for a different activity or I can choose healthy snacks such as fruit or raw vegetables. I have discovered that I also have choices about exercise. I can choose to force myself to engage in some type of exercise that will never motivate me or I can find an athletic activity that I enjoy. Enjoyable physical activity seems to reduce stress; thus, causing my desire to eat to lessen.

Educators have a difficult job. We should reward ourselves; few others will. However, our rewards should never come at the expense of our physical health. By making choices that are fun and healthy, we reduce risk to ourselves, we increase our energy, and we become models to our students of how to cope in a busy world while choosing a healthy lifestyle.

Chapter 12: Mental Health

Throughout my educational career, other teachers and I have often joked about needing a "mental health day". People in any job need time off for rest and relaxation. Teaching is stressful for many reasons, including oppositional students, non-supportive parents, a wide variation of colleagues, as well as a plethora of tasks and deadlines. After teaching for a while, you may feel the necessity of taking a "mental health day". However, you may discover that, as a first year educator, you do not have many personal days at your fingertips. If this is your situation or if you want to save your days for a later time, try giving an inexpensive gift to yourself every night of the week. On weekends, give yourself something extra special. Activities could include a hot bath, a massage by a spouse, a scented candle, an interesting novel, or an old movie. (These work for men as well as for women.) By patting yourself on the back, you will restore at least some of the sanity that you may have lost during the work day.

Chapter 13: Emotional Health

As a teacher, you will quickly learn that the emotional state of your students directly affects how well instruction can be delivered. If you have had a school disaster or if a few of your students are fighting, it is unlikely that the educational experience will be beneficial in that moment. The same is true for you. If you are hurt, angry, or fearful, it is unlikely that your instructional day will be a success. You will find that your best days of teaching are the days when you are at your happiest. Therefore, it is important that you always support your own emotional health, both for your sake and for the sake of your students.

During my first few years of teaching, I faced several emotional challenges that could have crippled my career. The first challenge that I faced was my classroom management. This is often one of the largest tests of a new teacher's staying power. When I saw that my discipline plan was less than perfect, I began to feel like a failure as a teacher. This feeling was sometimes supported by negative remarks of fellow staff members.

My next mountain to climb included my relations with parents. Although most of my students' parents supported me, there were always a few that challenged my authority. Over time, I learned that these same parents also had difficulty dealing with previous teachers, principals, and with anyone whose opinions differed from theirs.

In addition, there were also fellow staff and faculty who were less than positive. Joining a teaching staff (as obtaining any other job) presents its own rewards and challenges. You are the newcomer on the block and some are not sure whether you deserve to be a part of the group.

What I soon learned is that everyone makes mistakes, especially in the beginning of an adventure. I have certainly made my share. At the same time, everyone has personal, emotional issues to deal with. While you will no doubt make your share of mistakes, so will others. Fellow staff may make negative remarks, but you must weigh what is said. Use your own mental filters to protect yourself from unnecessary hurt and disappointment. We are all human; therefore, what we say is rarely perfect. Over time, you will have a feel for the climate of your campus. Either you will find yourself in a healthy, supportive workplace with a few negative souls or you will discover an unhealthy, controlled workplace where the administrators and the staff are seriously dysfunctional. Either way, you can learn from the experience and grow as a person in the midst of it.

There is one final thought that I feel is necessary to share regarding emotional health and teaching. In my own experience, I not only found that teaching gave opportunity for growth through present experiences, but growth in past issues as well.

During my first teaching experience, I taught special education. This sometimes required diapering young children, as well as any number of special diets, medical procedures by the school nurse, and numerous wheelchairs and other necessary adaptive equipment. My Dad had been seriously ill for ten years and had recently passed away prior to me obtaining my first teaching job. I found that the daily necessities of the physical care of these children were slowly taking a toll on my emotions because I had not fully recovered from all of the horrific experiences of my Father's illness.

Later in my career, I taught older students. Some of my preteen students were going through the roller coaster social experiences that puberty brings. I found myself constantly wanting to protect them from disappointment and pain. Unknowingly, I often took their stresses home with me and felt as if they were my own. It was not until I realized that I was feeling a sense of personal rejection from my own childhood school experiences that I realized that the pain that I was feeling belonged to me rather than them. Once I took ownership of my own pain, I began to see objectively through my emotions to the degree that I could truly assist them in their times of crises.

In essence, you may find that whatever unresolved issues linger from your own childhood may re-surface when you begin teaching. There is something about staring into those young faces every day that will force the child in you to the forefront. If you begin to have unexplained negative emotions, ask yourself what you are really feeling. Keep a private journal. If you continue to feel this way, seek help. We are in a helping profession. The best way to emotionally support others is to begin by supporting ourselves.

Chapter 14: Spiritual Health

The basis for success in any task is not the outer appearance, but lies in the matters of the human heart. We can be the best educator, the best attorney, the best physician, or the best parent by the world's standards; however, if we do not feel good about who we are as a person, the joy of that success is short-lived.

I am learning, with each new day, not to base my worth on my successes and failures, nor on my ability to please others. I believe that I was created by a Heavenly Father who loves me unconditionally. He is willing to forgive my shortcomings and is more than able to strengthen me for the next steps in my life's journey.

Therein is my comfort. Administrators, students, parents, and colleagues will disappoint you at times. In some situations, you will disappoint yourself. However, I have always relied on my spiritual walk to hold me in place when everything around me seems to crumble.

This was especially true when the September 11th tragedy took place. I was in my classroom teaching four year old children when a staff member came in to share the pieces of news with me that she had gathered. I misunderstood and thought that the Dallas/Ft. Worth metropolis was in imminent danger. For about 30 minutes, I was convinced that we were all going to die. At the same time, I had a peace that everything would be alright, whether we lived or not. I continued to teach, later learning that the whole event had taken place in New York City. When I entered teaching, I never dreamed that I would face such a horrible day while managing students and instruction. I believe that I triumphed in my circumstance because I have a loving Heavenly Father who will see me through anything.

As I have stated earlier in the book, no one can give to students what they do not possess. You can give them your physical energy, your mental abilities, and your emotional support. However, your greatest gift to them is yourself. At the center of your being, you must believe, with all of your heart, that you are valuable and that you have something great to give to others. When you can love your students unconditionally (not for what they can do, but for who they are), you are truly a teacher.

Concluding Remarks

Throughout this book, I have shared several of my own personal experiences, most of which took place early in my teaching career. Since that time, I have earned a graduate degree, taught a few more years, and have gained a tiny insight regarding what it means to effectively manage a campus, especially in the area of curriculum. When I was in the classroom, I easily blamed others for all of my stress. I constantly asked myself why this person required this and why that deadline was necessary. After all, do they not understand that I teach? It is true that teachers are often overworked because of all of the demands placed upon them. However, in this time that we live in, the same seems to be true for almost everyone, whether administrator, teacher, parent, student, or community member. The stress may not be worse or better than another, simply different.

It is my hope that while reading this book, you have gained some insight into the field of education, with both its rewards and its challenges displayed openly. Although I have worked feverishly on this book over weekends and holidays, it seems like I have spent many years writing it. Perhaps that is because I have been writing it mentally ever since I entered my first classroom. I began to quote that age old saying to myself, "I should write a book someday."

At the beginning of this school year, I took a position outside of the classroom. I am based on one campus, but I wear many hats. I assist teachers with curriculum needs, tutor students who are in need of assistance, assist with parent and community volunteer programs, and I also assist new teachers by providing them with training specific for the needs of incoming educators.

Being in this current position has caused me to see the necessity for not only informing new teachers of the policies and procedures of education, but introducing them to the hidden rules of success that are necessary for teachers throughout our nation's campuses to know. If we are to adequately prepare children to be leaders, we must be competent professionals of excellence! We must be confident, capable educators with both a goal for today and a vision for tomorrow.

Stephanie Smith

Many thanks to:

The Caterpillars, for being such a great team of folks and for inspiring me to press forward!

My friends in Spearhead, without whom I would never have had the boldness to achieve this goal,

My dining buddy, Dianne, who is a professional in the truest sense, but is also a great friend,

Tom and Pat, who have benefited me with their friendship, their encouragement, and their unique ability to conquer life's challenges,

Ken and Sue and their family, for being funny and encouraging,

My Parents, for loving Aaron and I, though we are very eccentric,

My Grandmother, who is a role model of strength and endurance,

My husband, Aaron, for being my best friend, my life companion, and a source of unconditional love,

My Creator and Heavenly Father, for being my ultimate source!

About the Author

Stephanie Smith has taught for ten years in Texas public schools. While teaching, she has served on Campus Improvement Committees, an Assessment Committee, and a Student Assistance Committee. She is also a campus representative for the Texas teacher evaluation system. She now works in Compensatory Education in North Texas, spending a portion of her time assisting in the mentorship of new teachers.

Stephanie began her journey toward the field of education with a B. S. in Education from UH-Clear Lake. She recently earned her Master's Degree in Educational Leadership and Policy Studies from the University of Texas in Arlington. She holds the following certifications:

Elementary Education, Special Education, ESL, Early

Childhood, English, and the Principalship.

www.ingramcontent.com/pod-product-compliance
Lightning Source LLC
Chambersburg PA
CBHW021546290526
45785CB00004BA/1759